Jamal's Creative Inspiration

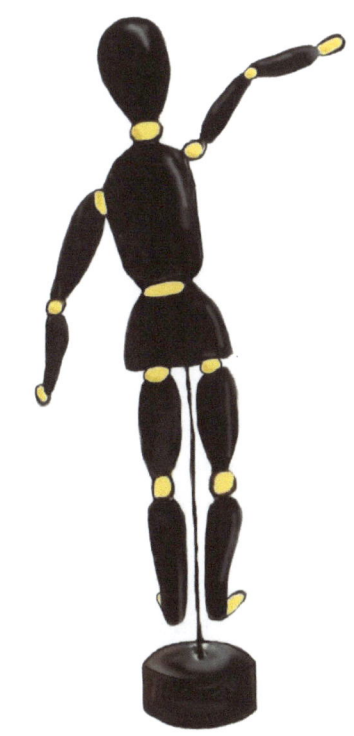

Alicia L. McDaniel

Published by Alicia McDaniel Fine Art in conjunction with
Art For the Creative Soul
Visit www.artforthecreativesoul.com today!

Summary: Jamal learns about seven renowned visual artists through conversations with people from his family and community.
ISBN: 978-0-9995573-1-0

For my family.

My name is Jamal and I love art. Photography is one of my favorite ways to express my creativity. I also love to study other kinds of visual expression. I read about many different artists. Learning about them inspires my creativity.

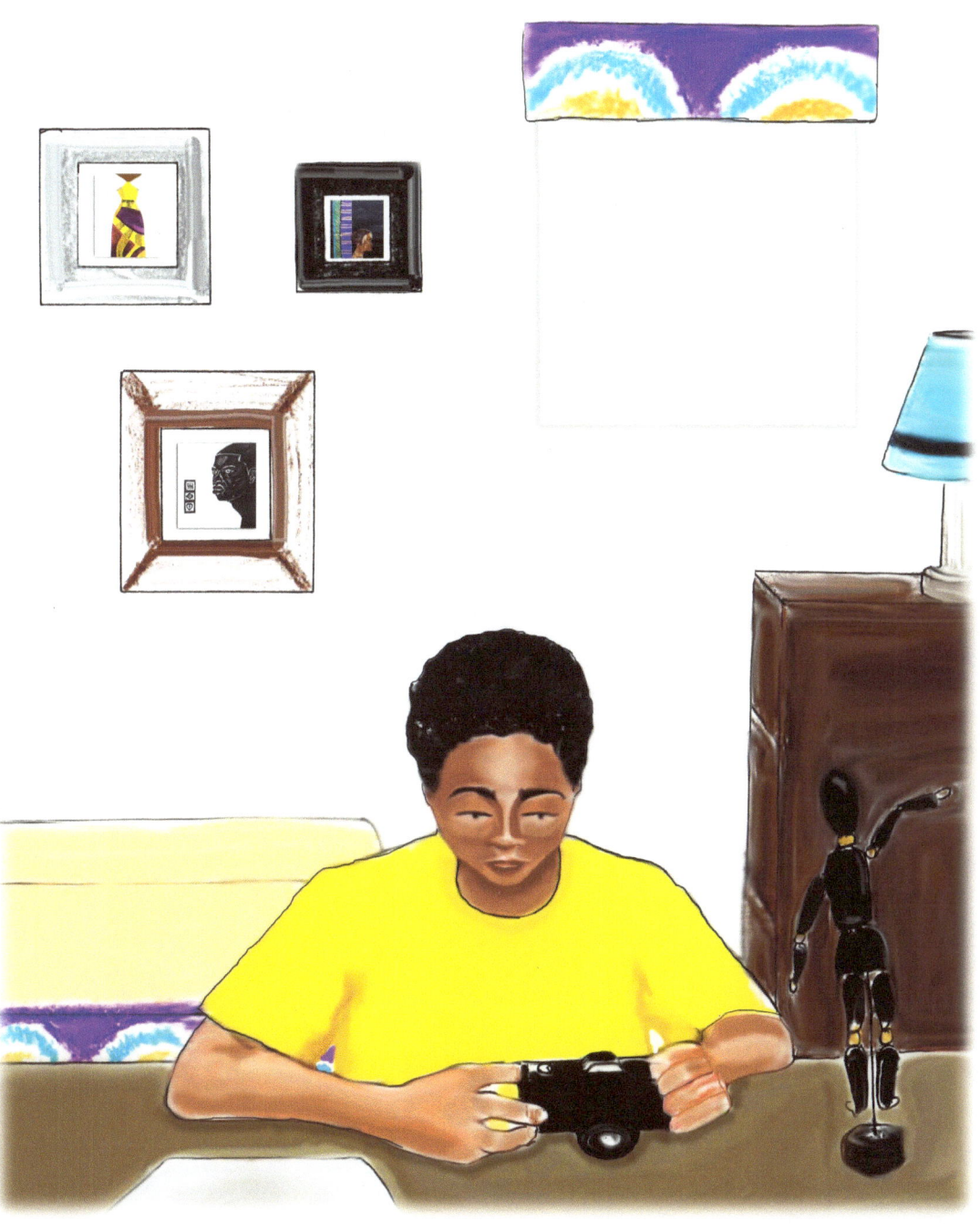

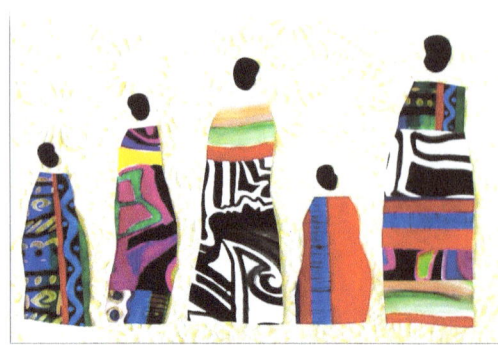

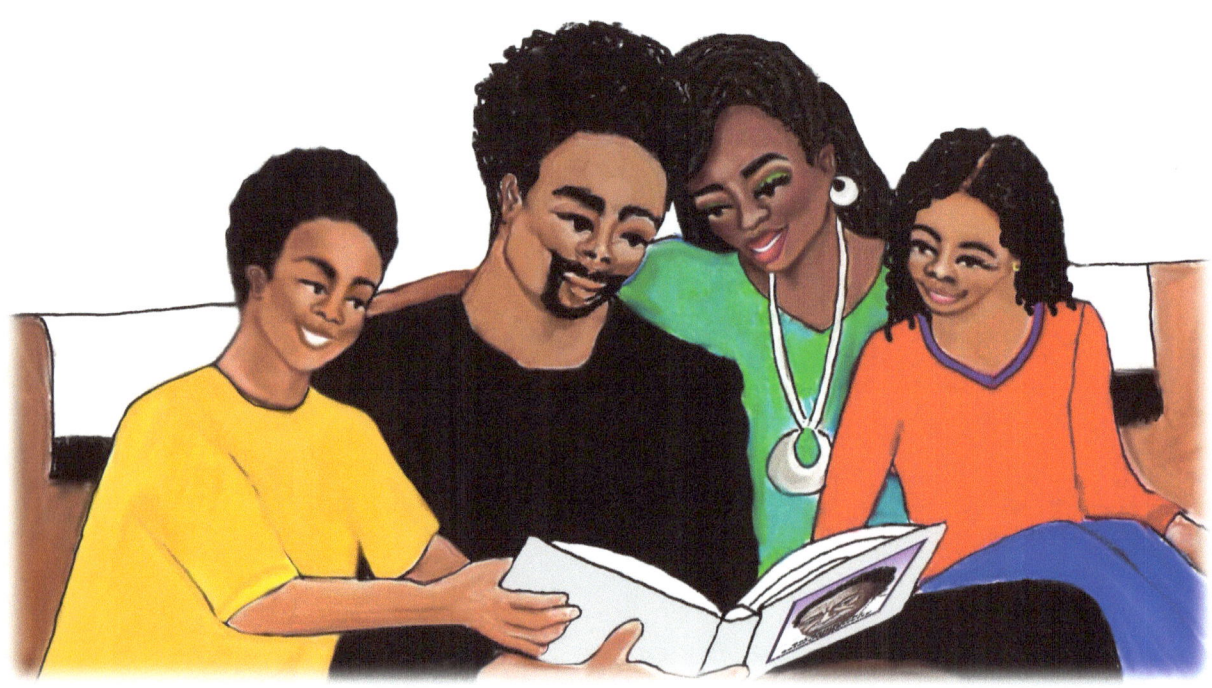

Every since we were very young, my parents have taught us about various visual artists. My sister Jamilah is also a talented artist. One of my favorite books that my father shared with us is about the renowned photographer, Gordon Parks.

Gordon Parks was a really cool artist. He was a famous photographer, film director, and author. He created a film called "The Learning Tree". When I take photographs, I think about his style and try to take photographs that look like his work.

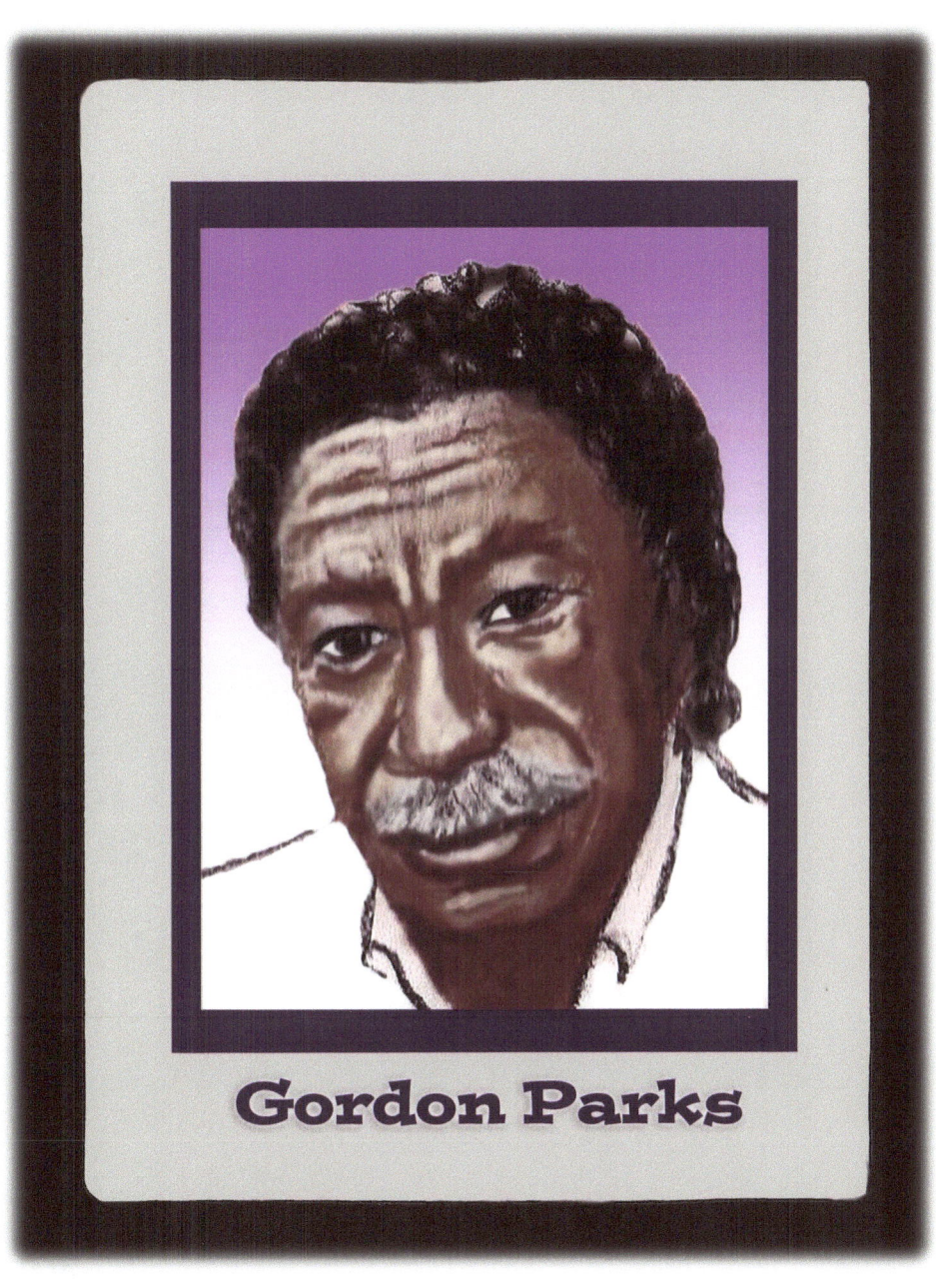

Gordon Parks

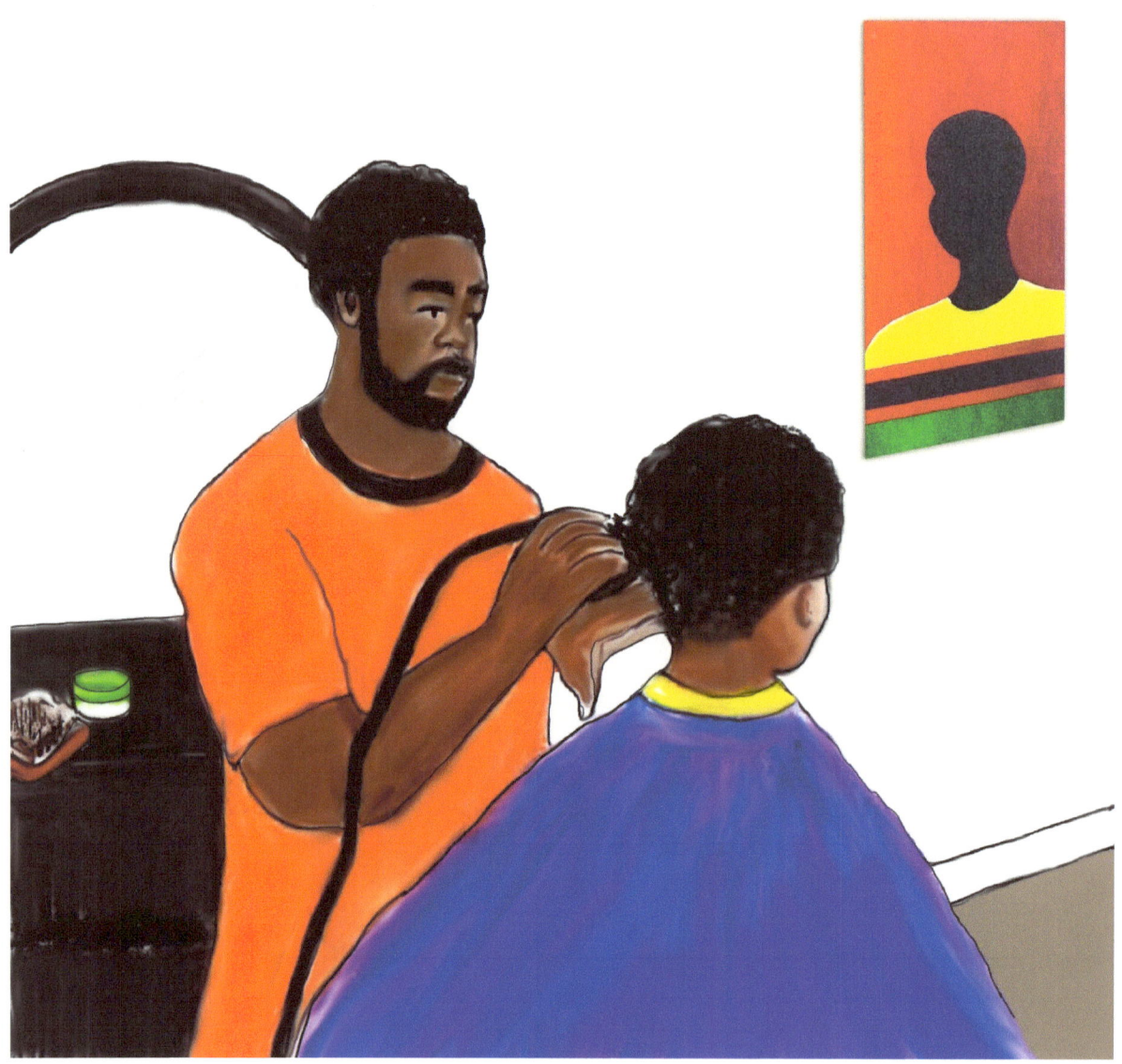

When I go to my uncle's barbershop, I always learn new things about art and life. My uncle minored in art history in college. The last time I got my hair cut, he told me about an artist named Sargent Claude Johnson.

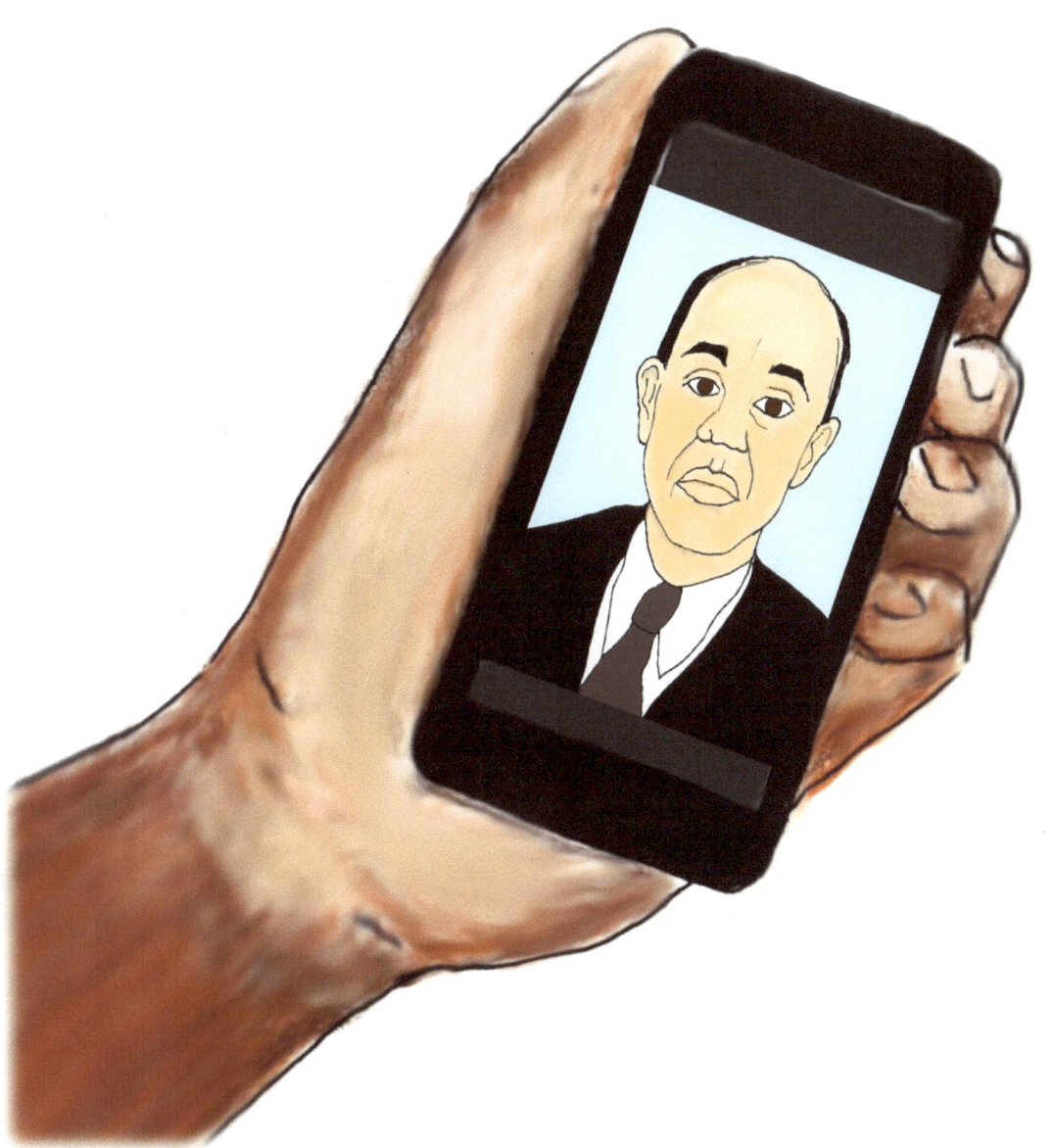

Sargent Claude Johnson was very diverse in his artistic expression. He was a printmaker, graphic designer, sculptor and painter. His sculptures are really unique. I like to create graphic designs too.

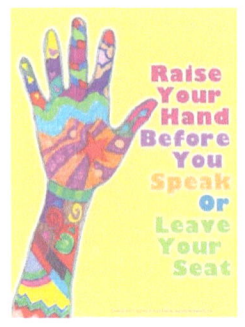

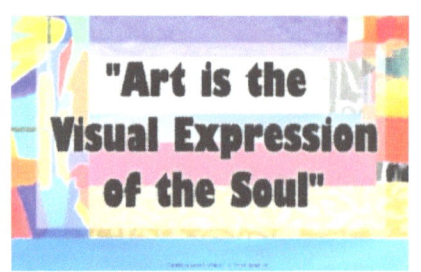

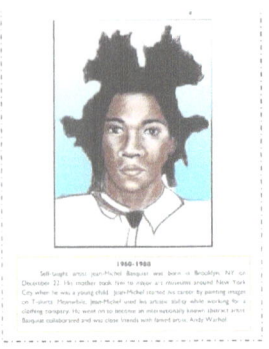

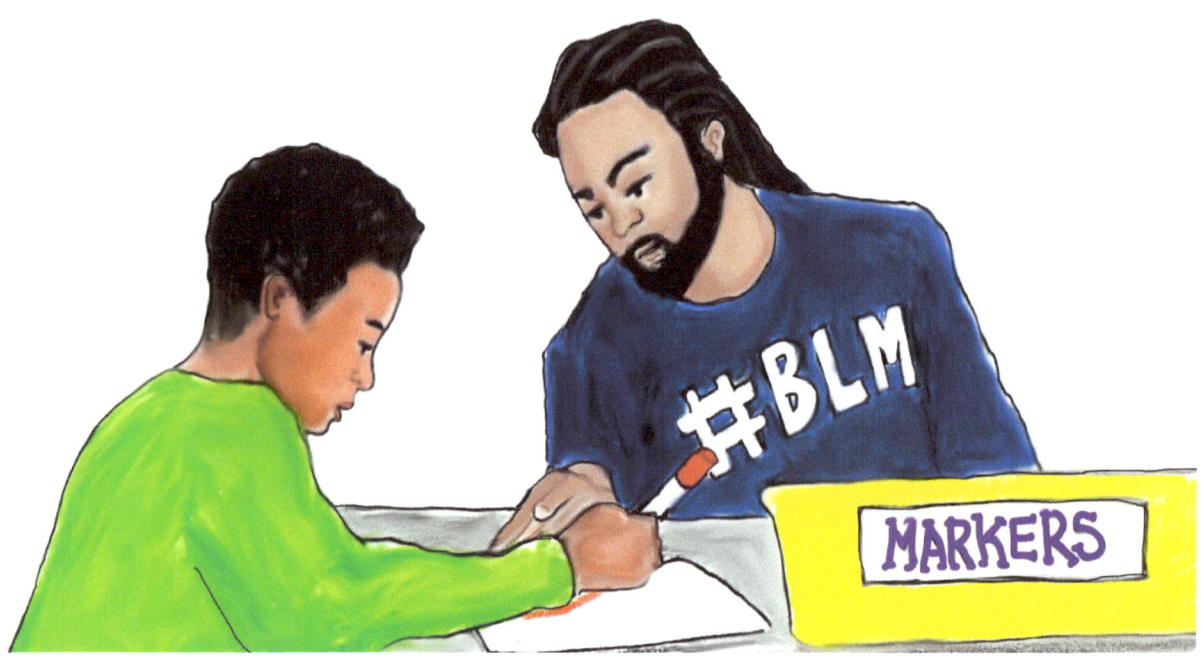

Fifth period is one of my favorite times of the day at school because it's when I go to my art exploration class. Our art teacher is named Mr. Smith. He encourages us to explore new ways to express our creativity. He also teaches us about significant artists such as, Jean-Michel Basquiat.

Jean-Michel Basquiat was a self-taught, abstract artist. He started his art career by creating t-shirt designs. His style of creating art was very bold and unique. Jean-Michel used a crown symbol in many of his abstract paintings. The crowns make his paintings feel regal.

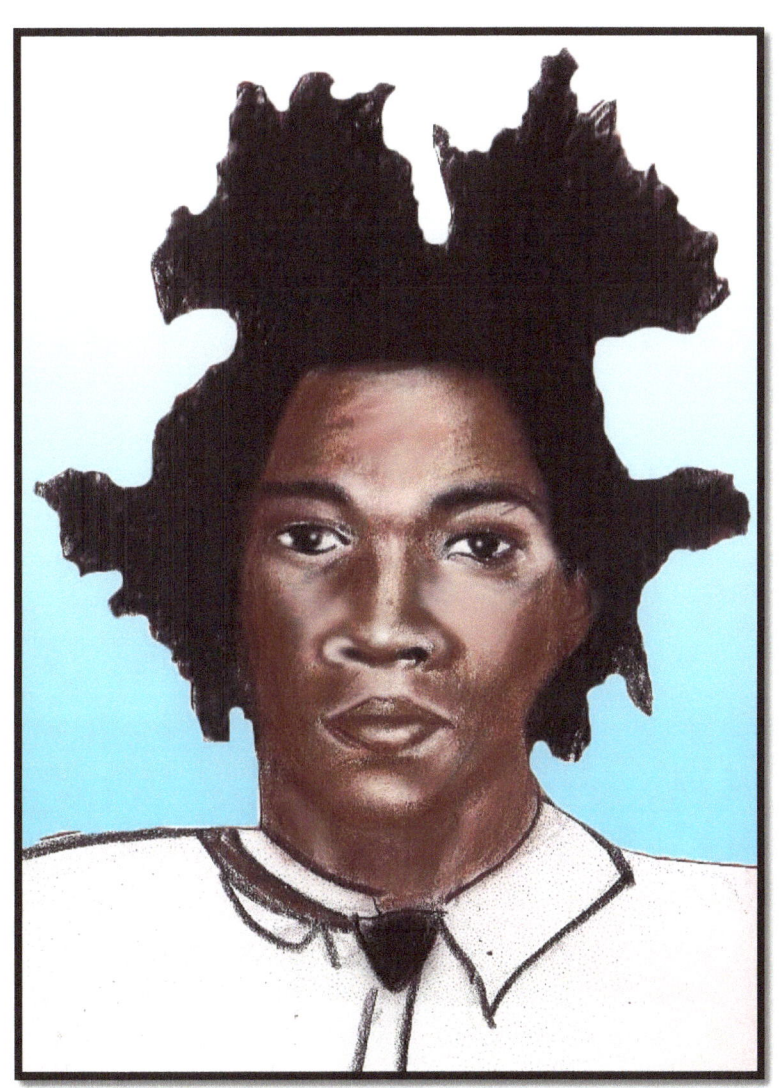

Every Saturday, I take private music lessons. I'm learning how to play the saxophone. My music teacher, Mr. Thomas, is a great musician. In his music studio, there is a portrait of the prolific artist, Romare Bearden.

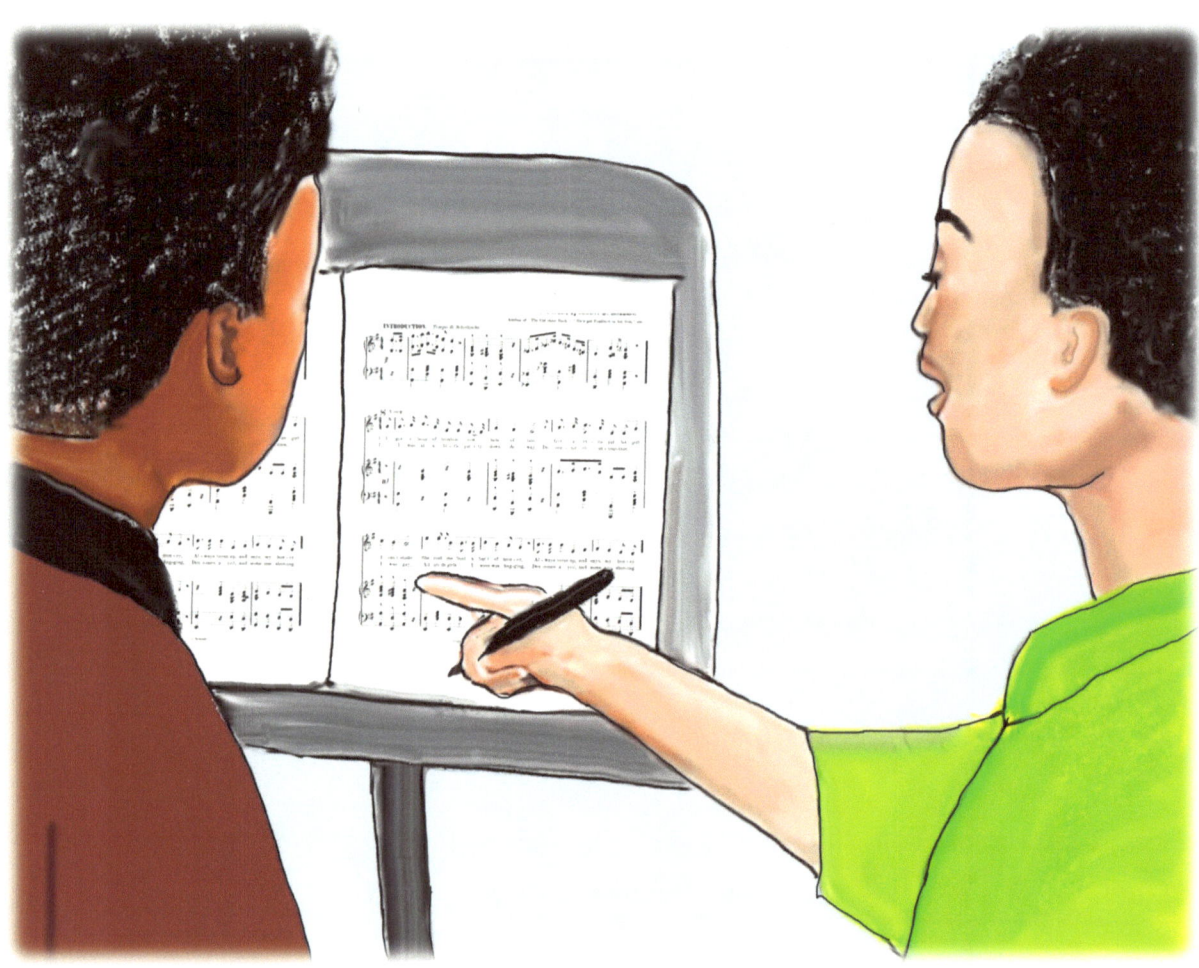

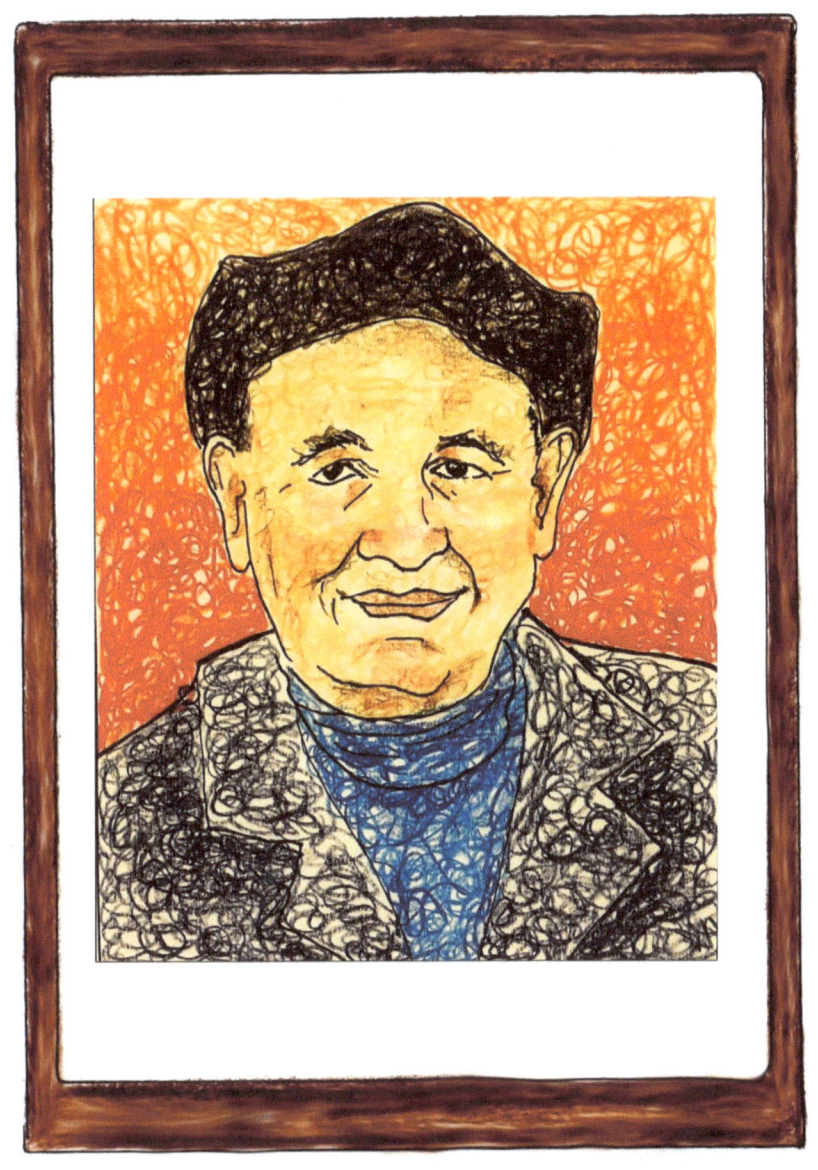

Romare Bearden created colorful collages and paintings inspired by our community. He also created art that focused on jazz music and musicians. Mr. Thomas told me that he worked as a social worker as well. I admire Mr. Bearden for having more than one profession.

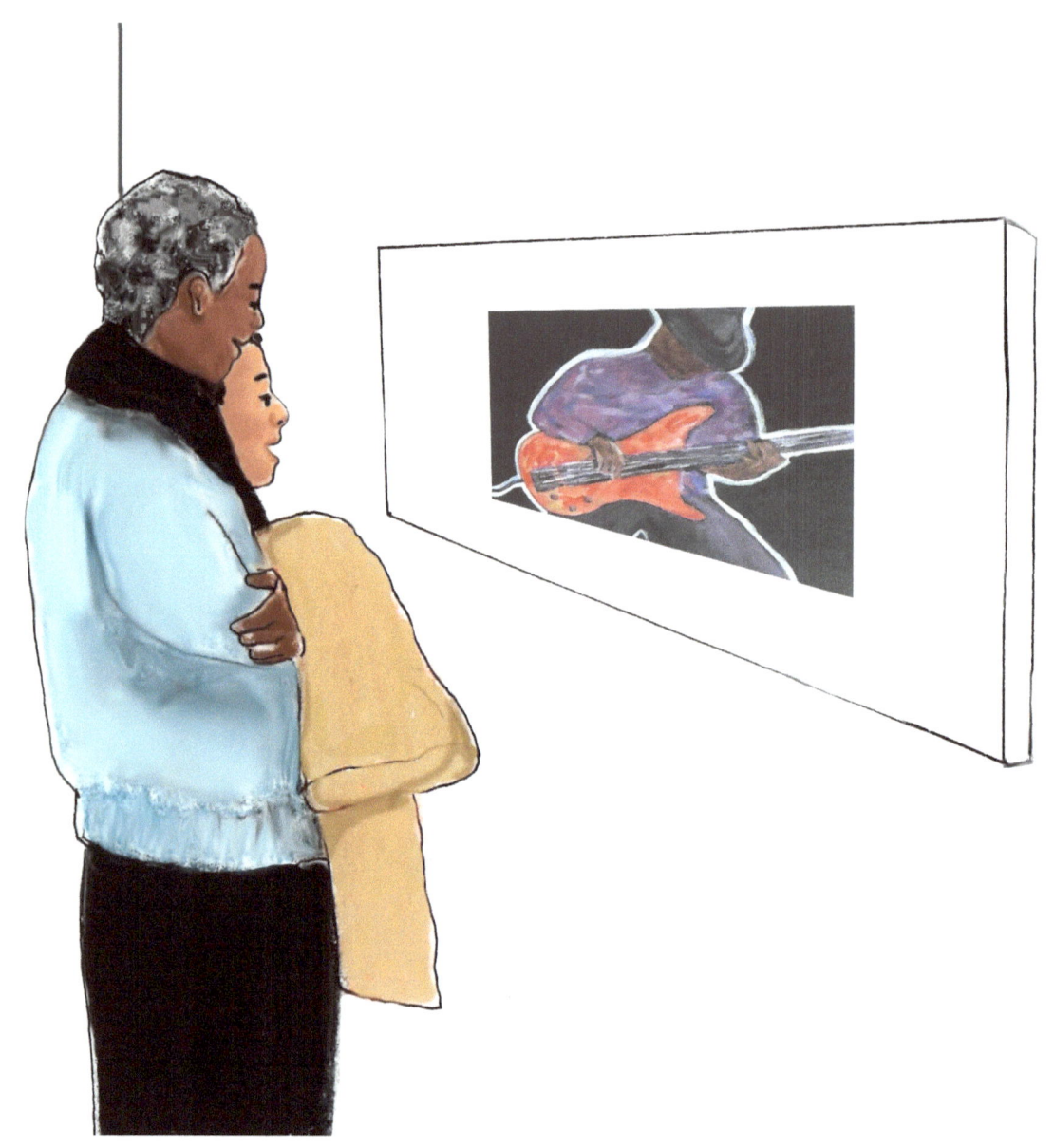

I really enjoy spending time with my grandfather. He is funny and smart. He takes me to places like the local African-American Cultural Center. The last time we went, I learned about the talented artist, Dr. John T. Biggers.

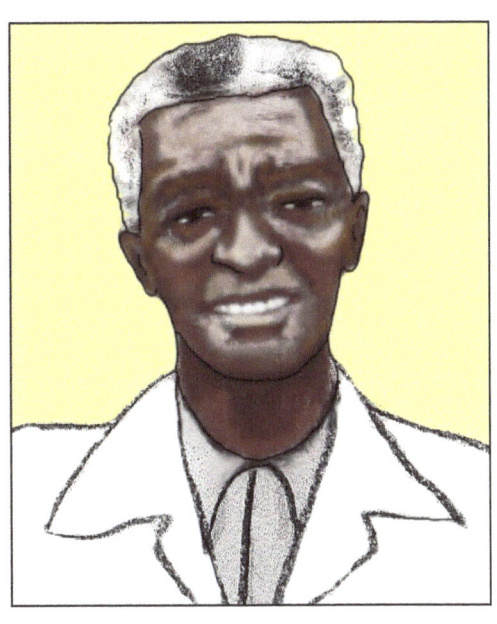

Sunday	Monday	Tuesday	Wednesday	Thursday	Friday	Saturday
		1	2	3	4	5
6	7	8	9	10	11	12
13 ⭐	14	15	16	17	18	19
20	21	22	23	24	25	26
27	28	29	30	31		

April

In the cultural center gift shop, I saw a calendar featuring Dr. Biggers. He established an art education program at Texas State University. Dr. Biggers also painted vibrant murals around Houston, TX and the United States. His art highlighted African-American culture.

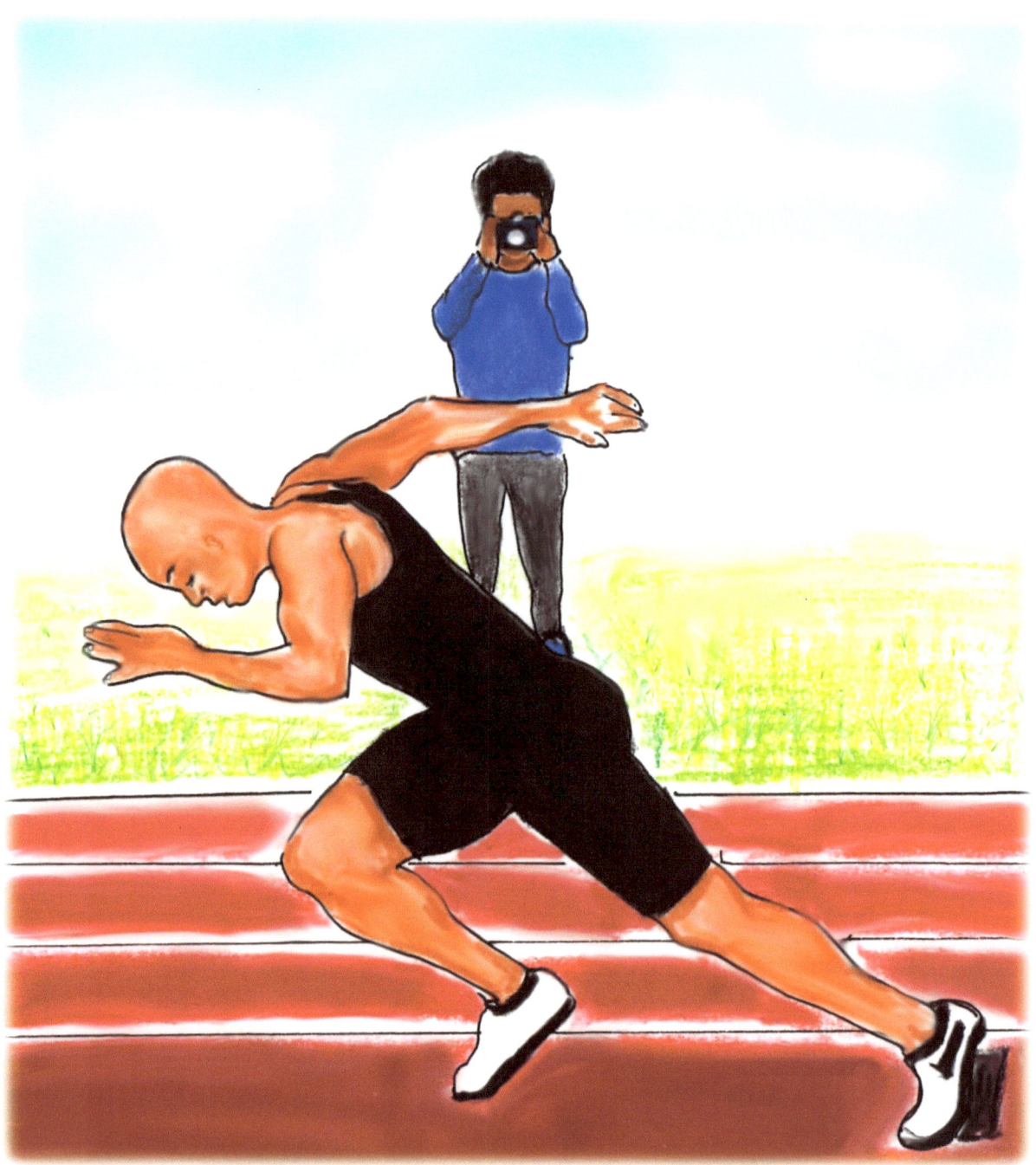

My cousin is a professional track athlete. Sometimes I photograph him while he practices for competitions. I recently saw a painting of runners in a race, on my computer. The famous artist, Jacob Lawrence, created the painting.

Jacob Lawrence was an award-winning artist who created colorful paintings of African-American life. His wife, Gwendolyn Knight, was also an artist. Jacob Lawrence was inspired by other visual artists from the Harlem Renaissance. He also liked to collect different types of tools.

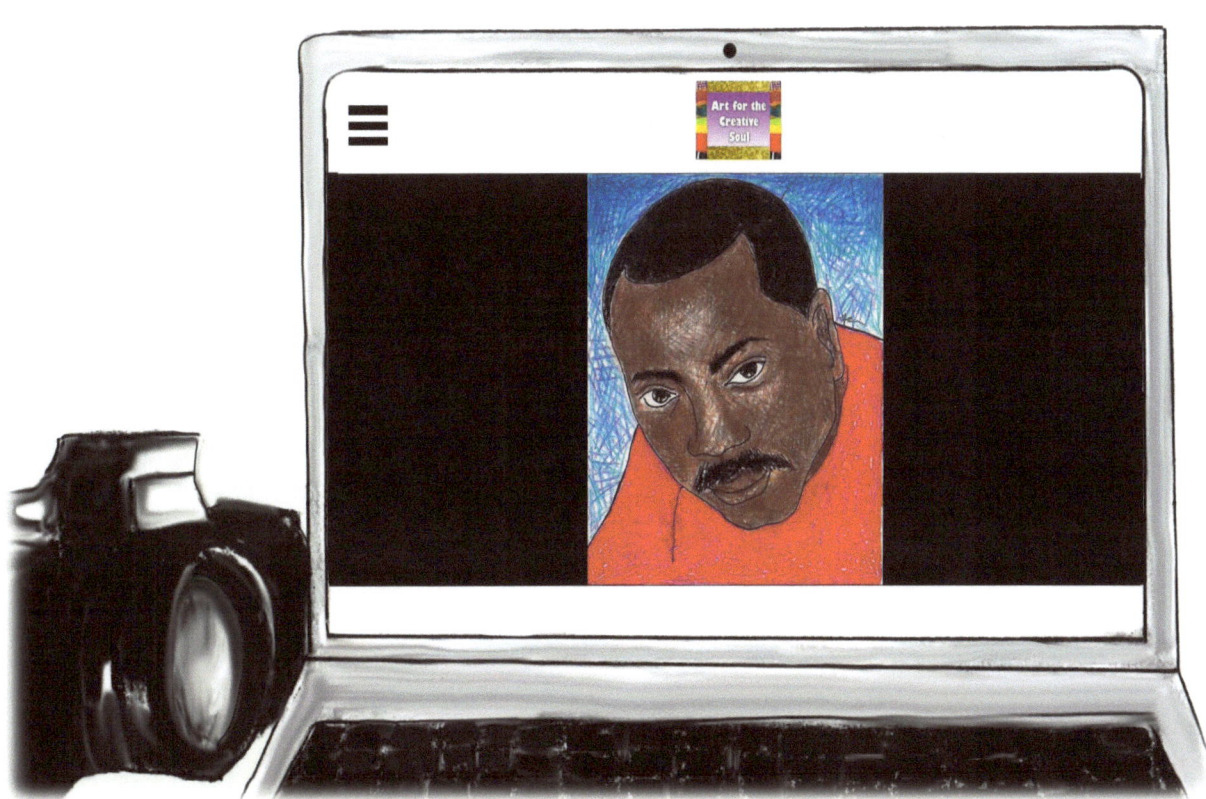

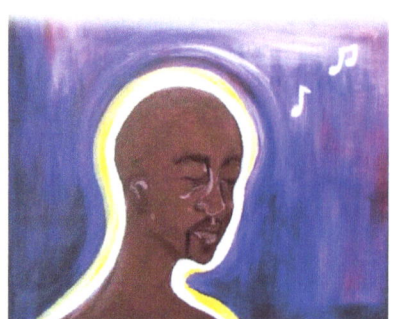

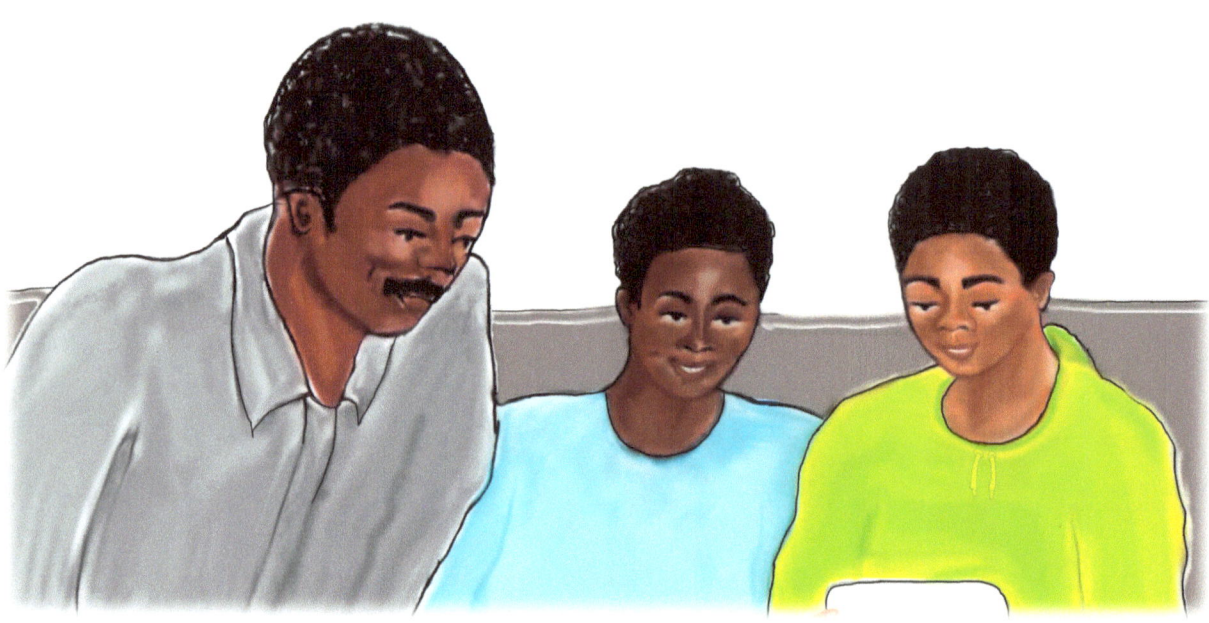

I hang out with my best friend Aaron almost every day. Aaron is also creative. His dad is a professional writer who likes to talk with us about important topics and people. He introduced us to an interesting visual artist named James A. Porter.

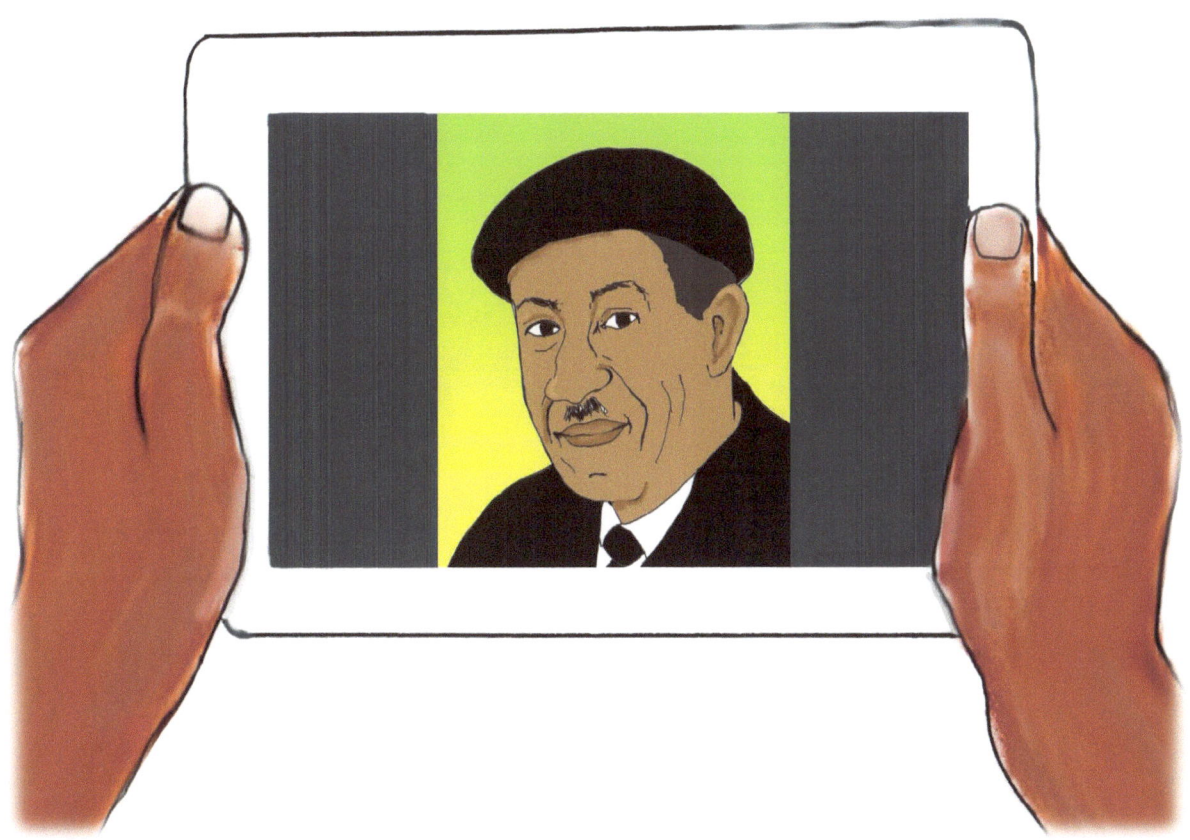

Mr. Porter was a visual artist, educator and art historian. After he graduated from college, he taught art and wrote an important book about African-American visual artists. My dad has a copy of the book in his office.

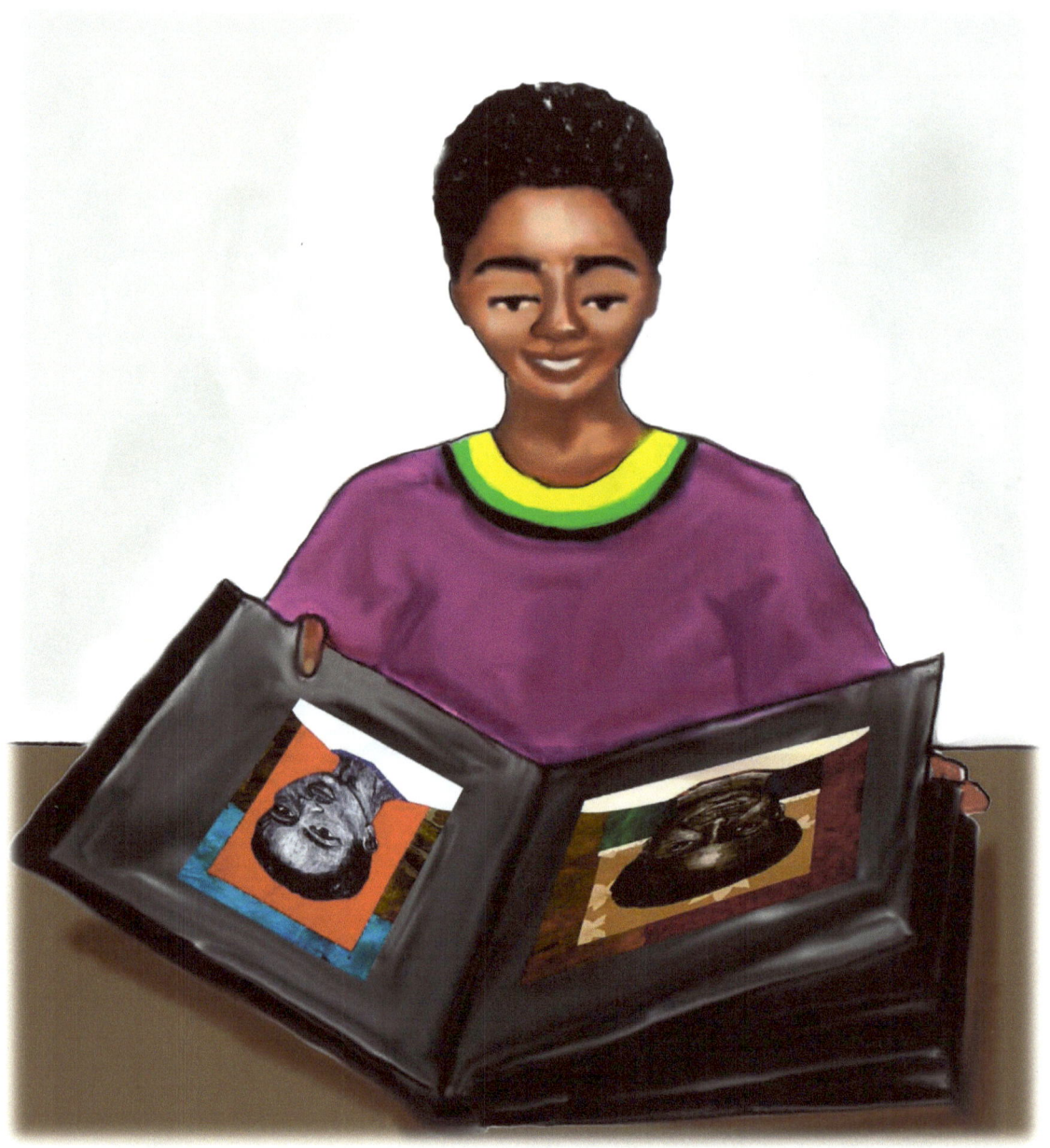

As I look through my art portfolio, I think about all of the amazing visual artists I've learned about so far. They created art that displays strength, beauty and inspiration. I will use my creativity to do the same thing.

Artist Gallery

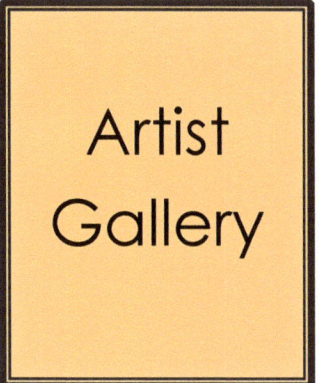

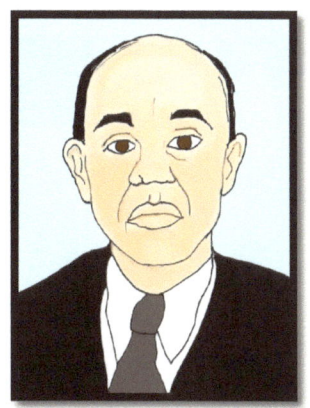

Sargent Claude Johnson
1888-1967

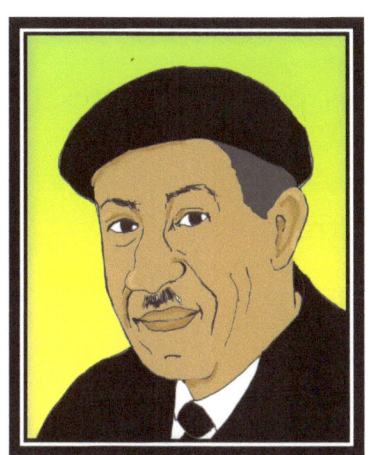

James A. Porter
1905-1970

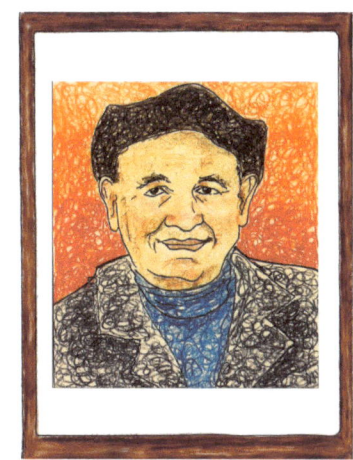

Romare Bearden
1911-1988

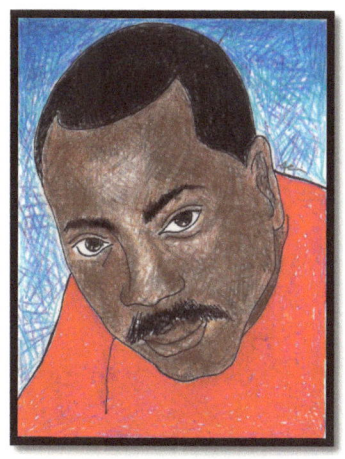

Jacob Lawrence
1917-2000

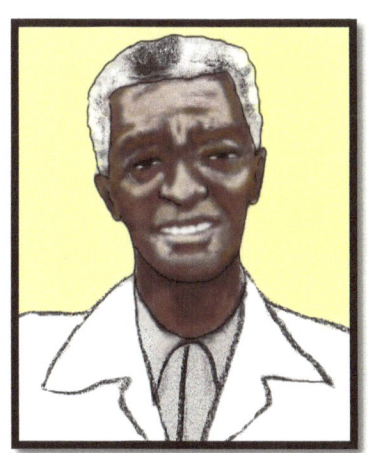

Dr. John T. Biggers
1924-2001

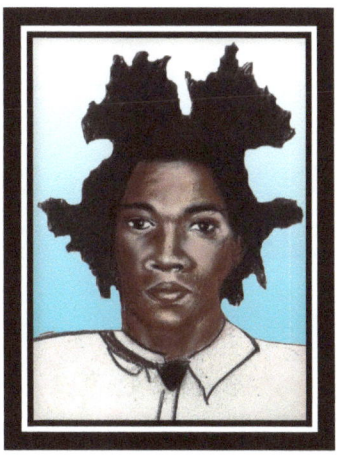

Jean-Michel Basquiat
1960-1988

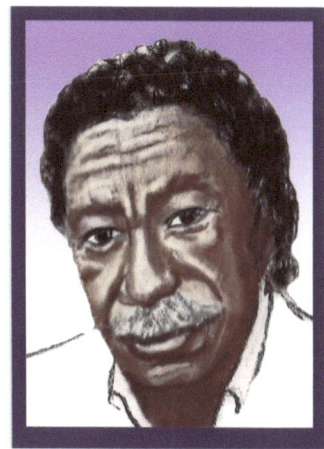

Gordon Parks
1912-2006

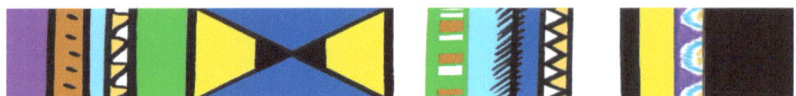

Art Glossary

Collage- Art made with cut and/or torn pieces of paper that are glued to another surface.

Expression- A way that an individual and/or group share ideas, thoughts and/or culture.

Graphic Design- A visual artist who creates logo designs, posters, websites, package designs, etc.

Mural- Art painted or drawn on the wall of a building or structure.

Portfolio- A collection of art.

Prolific- Productive or creative.

Vibrant- Full of energy.

Visual- An object created to be viewed with the eyes.

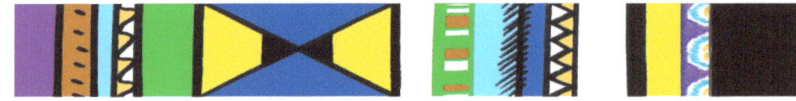

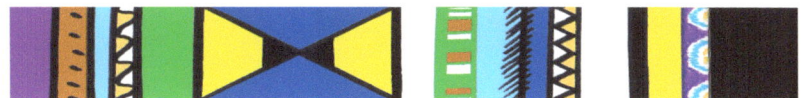

Discussion Questions

1. Jamal likes to take photographs. What is your favorite device to take photos with?

2. What is your favorite way to learn about topics you're interested in?

3. Jamal learned many facts about visual artists from his parents. What is something important that you learned from your parents?

4. Which artist in the story interests you the most? Why?

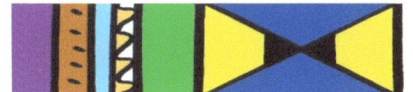
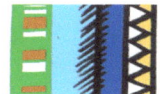
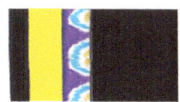

Alicia L. McDaniel is a professional artist, art educator and creative author. She enjoys creating art education products that celebrate the contributions of African-Americans to visual arts around the world.

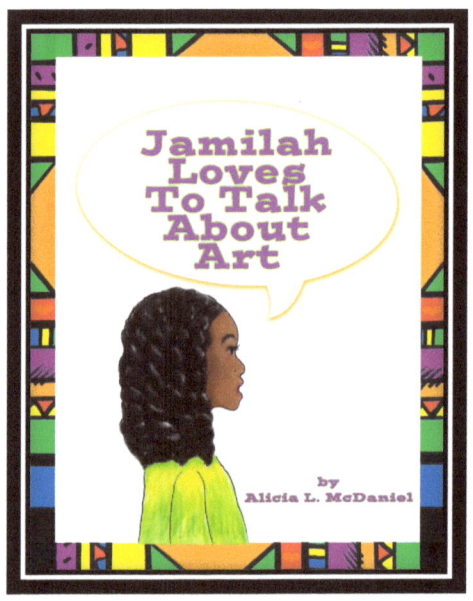

Make sure to get a copy of the companion book, Jamilah Loves to Talk About Art *today!!!*

These educational resources also feature the artists from the story. Visit www.artforthecreativesoul.com today!

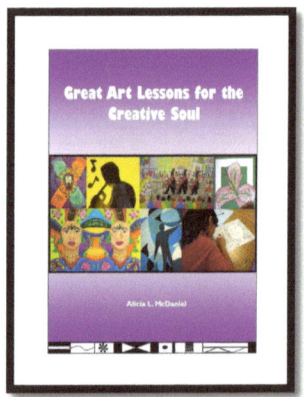

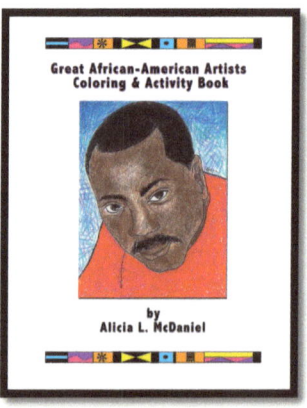

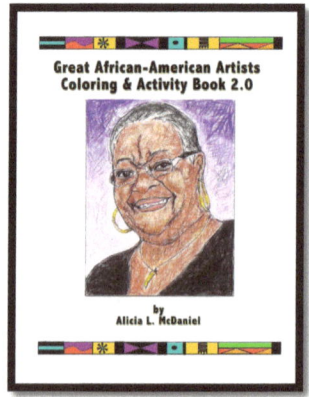

www.ingramcontent.com/pod-product-compliance
Lightning Source LLC
Chambersburg PA
CBHW050434180526
45159CB00006B/2529